Group Home Drama: Raven's Story

The names and identifying characteristics of some of the individuals in this book have been changed to protect their privacy.

Copyright © 2016 by M.C. Lishay

First Edition

All rights reserved. No part of this book may be reproduced, stored in a retrieval system, or transmitted by any form or by any means, electronic, mechanical, photocopying, recording, or otherwise, except as expressly permitted by the applicable copyright statutes or in writing by the Publisher.

Published in the United States of America.

For information, contact publisher@elitelifeskills.com.

Library of Congress Cataloguing-in-Publication Data has been applied for.

ISBN: 978-0-692-78144-9

And we know that all things work together for good to them that love God, to them who are the called according to his purpose.

- Romans 8:28

The Critical Tape

~

I always tell my clients about the "Critical Tape" which is a metaphor for those negative thoughts that start to play in our head when we are feeling depressed, defeated, or insecure about ourselves. We will never be able to completely stop this tape from playing due to certain situations that arise in our lives (for instance, the death of a loved one, a break up, or unfulfilled goals) but we do have the ability to pause it for long periods of time once we are equipped with the knowledge, tools, and techniques needed to do so.

- M.C. Lishay

Acknowledgments

~

While growing up, I had to overcome a lot of challenges in my life that left me questioning God as to why I was chosen to endure so much pain and suffering. I wondered why I couldn't just be a normal person - a person with a normal job, a normal life, or a normal family. Then one day as I was lying in my bed listening to my critical tape crying about how depressing and sad my life was, it hit me. God puts certain individuals through certain things because they are strong enough to handle them and because we are meant to be a blessing to others.

I know when other people look at me they think my life is pretty damn great. After all, I have a beautiful son who loves me; a family that has always been there for me; a beautiful home in a beautiful neighborhood; and a nice car. To the average person I'm living the so called "American Dream." But it was anything but that to me. Have you ever heard the expression that you can be in a room full of people who love you and care about you and feel totally alone? That's how I felt for the longest.

I mean, after all, I was empty on the inside but I knew what the issue was. See, I am one of those people who for whatever reason God decided to bless with many gifts. I am what you would call a "Jack of all trades." The problem with being multi-skilled is that you are never really happy or content in any job because you get bored easily and have this need to use all the gifts that God has blessed you with. The other issue is that you tend to get laid off a lot (not fired) because people think you want their job when that is the furthest thing from the truth.

Throughout all of these struggles, I have to thank my sister because without her I think I would be in a psychiatric ward right about now. She is able to do what my parents cannot which is to make me focus and refuse to give up on myself. To tell the truth, she acts more like my mother than anything else. Don't get me wrong. I love and respect my mother and father but they have never been as hard on me as my sister has and is. I dedicate this book to my sister; without her this book would have never been written. I also would like to dedicate this book to all of the youth who have inspired this book series. The one thing that I can truly say is that the youth that I talk about in this book series have gone through things that should have broken them into a million pieces but didn't. Because of that, they are truly my inspiration.

The first youth that you will learn about is Raven. Her real name and other identifying information have been changed to protect her privacy. I chose to write my first book about Raven because she is the first youth that I met over 20 years ago who made a huge impression on me. I hope she makes the same impression on you. All 10 of the books that I have written are based on true stories. I wanted to tell you about each one of the youth's stories because sometimes we go through things and do not understand why we were chosen to go through them. So, we feel like giving up because we just don't see the point of it all anymore.

Well, I am here to let you know that the youth that you will be reading about have been through things that I know will have some of you in open mouth shock and wondering why they didn't give up on not only themselves but on life in general. But I am here to tell you, it gets better. I know it all sounds cliché but it really does. Even though it might not ever seem like it will be, it does. There are individuals like myself who were truly put here on earth to help people in situations like this and who will give you a whole new perspective on, not just your life but life itself.

So when you read my books, take your time. Put yourself in these youths' shoes. Take time out to think about what happened in each chapter and how you would have dealt with the situations. Ask questions and send them to me at ask@elitelifeskills.com. Start a journal and think about the pros and cons when dealing with certain situations. Think about how each youth's choices affected other people around them. Get angry, cry, and have discussions about these youths. That's the point and the reason that I wrote these books. Some people may see these books as self-help guides to overcome or deal with certain situations. Some may see these books as life lines, and then others may see these books as pure entertainment.

No matter how these books affect you or how you look at them just remember one thing. These are real teenagers who have gone through some very real and unfortunate situations.

Table of Contents

~

Acknowledgments..................................-05-

Forward...-14-

Safe Haven's Map Site..........................-19-

Introduction...-20-

Chapter 1
The Beginning......................................-32-

Chapter 2
The Situation.......................................-49-

Chapter 3
Raven Who?...-68-

Chapter 4
This is Staff...-97-

Chapter 5
The Raid...-105-

Chapter 6
Therapy Time……………………………….-119-

Chapter 7
The Church Experience………………….-131-

Chapter 8
My First Real Kiss……………………………-143-

Chapter 9
The New Girl……………………..…..……..-150-

Chapter 10
The Fight Within………………..…..……..-163-

Chapter 11
Safe…………………………………………….-169-

Chapter 12
The Here and Now………………………….-176-

Foreword

~

My name is M.C. Lishay. For more than 20 years, I have provided individual and group counseling to children and adolescents in transitional living programs, group homes, shelters, and foster care homes while working under the direct supervision of licensed clinical professional counselors and clinical psychologists. I have worked with families and children who have been diagnosed with almost everything in the *Diagnostic and Statistical Manual of Mental Disorders, Fifth Edition, DSM-5*, by the American Psychiatric Association. That includes everything from autism to schizophrenia.

I am highly educated in the child welfare field, earning the following degrees and certification from Roosevelt University in Chicago, Illinois: a Bachelor of Arts degree in psychology; a Master of Arts degree in clinical professional psychology; and a graduate certificate in Clinical Child and Family Studies. I also have studied at the Illinois School of Professional Psychology, now Argosy University. I am also a licensed Child Welfare Service Employee (CWEL) and hold a Childhood Severity of Psychiatry Illinois (CSPI) Graham Certificate from Northwestern University Feinberg School of Medicine, Department of Psychiatry and Policy Program. Due to my frequent contact with families and juvenile courts, I later earned certification as a paralegal from DePaul University.

For the most part, I have loved working with children, adolescents, and even their families. The reason that I say for the most part is because once in a while you will have the pleasure of working with a child who comes with a family that loves to keep up a lot of unnecessary drama. These are the families with whom I least like working.

I feel like the family should come to therapy wanting to do what is in the best interests of the child/youth and their family. But drama-based families want all of the attention on them, don't care about the child's well-being, or don't want to help the child to deal with their issues.

Due to the instability I have encountered while working in the social services field, I decided to start my own business called Elite Life Skills Coaching. Elite is a nationwide organization which helps individuals deal with life challenges. Elite allows me to coach individuals face-to-face, by phone, web conference, or e-mail. Sometimes, I fly to other states to coach individuals, conduct lectures, and participate in speaking engagements. I offer meetings/trainings on a variety of topics such as "Time Management," "How to Deal with Depression," "Holiday Blues," and "Married Couples Issues."

Since I have started Elite I have felt complete. People from all walks of life can meet with me in a confidential setting without the fear of someone finding out about their sessions.

For more information about Elite, go to www.elitelifeskills.com.

Safe Haven's Map Site

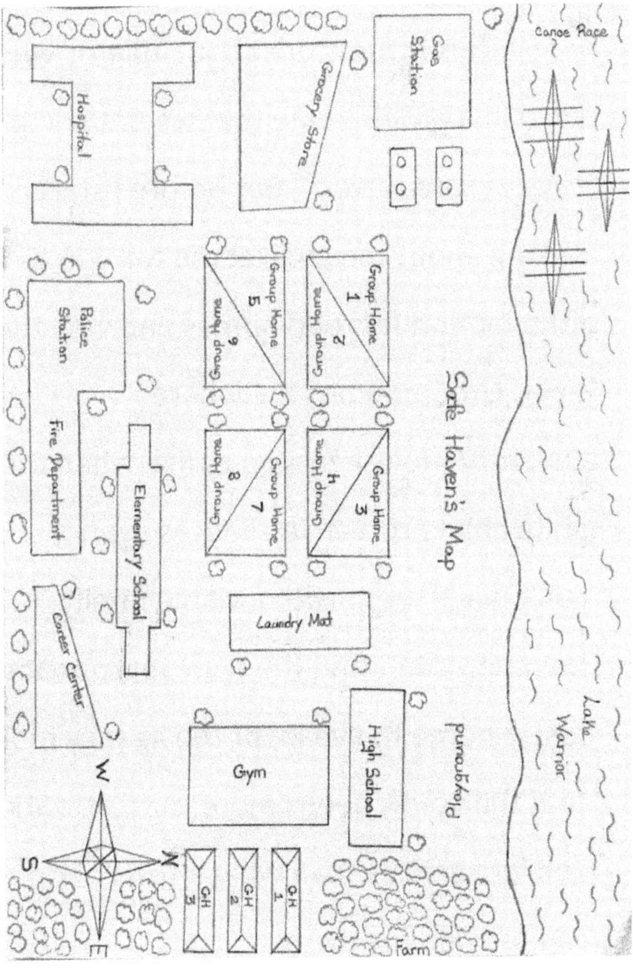

Introduction

~

This is the story about 10 girls who lived in a group home that we are going to call "Safe Haven." But before I start talking about the girls let me tell you a little bit about group homes and why they exist. Group homes are where children/adolescents go to live when the state child protective services agency can't place them with a viable family member, can't find them an appropriate foster home to live in, or the agency feels that the youth needs more care, attention and/or services than what a foster home can provide for them.

Did you know that the number of youth in foster care in the United States is over 400,000, according to www.fosterclub.com. Only around 100,000 of these children/adolescents end up getting adopted which means that about 1 in 184 children/adolescents in the United States are in a foster home. The average age of a child entering the foster care system is around 8.9 years of age. Fifty-two percent are boys, while 48 percent are girls. So where do all of these children/adolescents end up living? Four percent are in pre-adoptive homes; 29 percent are in foster family homes (relatives); 46 percent are in foster family homes (non-relatives); 6 percent are in group homes; 8 percent are in institutions; 1 percent are in supervised independent living arrangements; 1 percent are runaways; and 5 percent are in trail homes.

Typically, there are eight to 16 youths in one group home, and there is at least one trained caregiver for every four youths. Normally the ratio is 1:4 in children group homes but once in a while you might get a youth that needs or requires a 1:1 ratio due to his or her suicidal or homicidal behaviors. Most youth end up in group homes as a last result. Some youth are placed in a group home when they come into child protective service's care due to the nature of the situation they were involved in and what kind of care they need due to that situation. Such situations include: a youth that has been sexually abused and has become a sexual abuser himself or herself. This youth would be placed in a Sexual Assault Survivor Youth (SASY) group home. A youth that is Developmentally Delayed (DD) would be placed in a DD group home. Other situations include the age of the youth, sex of the youth, and behaviors.

    The facility that I use to work at, Safe Haven, is located in the middle of nowhere in the Midwest. The reason that I say it is located in the middle of nowhere is because of the fact that if one of the youths decided that he or she wanted to go "on-run" they had a long way to go before they reached a populated area. By the way, "on-run" means that a youth decides that he or she wants to leave the group home and go, for instance, to the city on a hike to cool off from a heated argument or situation, to party, or smoke. Runners go on-run for a number of reasons, but it was almost impossible because of how far they would have to walk before they saw a car or people. Safe Haven sits on 120 acres of land. It is like a town all by itself. There is a hospital, fire station, police station, elementary school, and a high school. Also, there is a gym, a grocery store, a gas station, a few green houses, a farm, a couple of parks, a nice lake that the youth had canoe races on, a huge laundry mat, and a career center where youths go to learn how to do different jobs and to get jobs on campus. As I said, Safe Haven was a town all by itself.

I must say, looking back on everything now, I loved working at Safe Haven. Let me be more specific. I actually loved working with the youth and helping them to achieve their goals and overcome their fears and past traumatic experiences or negative situations. Some of the staff, on the other hand, I really didn't care for because they engaged in a lot of unethical behavior that should have resulted in them being fired, losing their license, or being incarcerated. You will understand what I mean by this in a little while. Throughout my book series, you are going to read about different staff members not only doing unethical things but criminal things as well.

Now don't get me wrong. Some staff members who work in the group homes are actually there because they want to help the youth. As a matter of fact, some of the staff members I knew were examples of individuals whom the youth could relate to since the staff members overcame similar obstacles. I loved working with and talking to these staff members because I knew that their hearts were really into the profession. Let's take Tasha, for example.

Tasha came into my office one day upset about something that one of the girls had said to her.

The girl told her, "You don't understand what the fuck I'm going through. You get to go home every damn night."

Tasha informed me that she knows what these girls are going through, and it upsets her when one of the girls speaks to her like that.

Tasha stated that when she was 12 years old her mother fell in love with this so called "man of her dreams" but that the man of her dreams turned out to be an "asshole" as well as a pedophile.

Tasha said that from the time she turned 13 years old until her 19th birthday she was being sexually abused by this man.

I asked her if she ever said anything to her mother about it. "Of course, I did. I told her several times but she didn't believe me," replied Tasha.

Instead, Tasha's mom asked her, "What did you do Tasha?"

Tasha told me that the abuse stopped when she turned 19 and moved in with a friend of hers.

Tasha then said, "I think you know my friend. She works in "Group Home 3" with the SASY girls."

Tasha was right. I did know who her friend was because I know that girl's story as well. Tasha's friend was getting physically and sexually abused by her father, too. As I said before, I loved working with staff members who related to the group home children because I knew that they really cared about the youth with whom they worked.

However, you had some staff members who will tell you, "I'm working this job because it's easy money, and there is nothing hard about babysitting a few kids."

Do you know that every single time that I heard that line or someone say "All you do is baby-sit," I laugh to myself because they are in for a hell of a surprise.

I must say though, the craziest thing that I've ever heard a staff member say was that they were working at Safe

Haven because it was their way of keeping these "little ass niggas" in check (a white male staff member actually said this). Let me make this absolutely clear. This statement was never said directly to me because if it had been .... well that's a whole different story. But you will hear more about this staff member later and find out what happened to this staff member whom I will call Tom.

I decided to write the "Group Home Book Series" because I think about these girls every day. I think about what happened to them, where they are, what goals they have accomplished, whether they had any kids, and the number of kids they actually had. But the thing I think about the most is ... did I really help them as much as I could have.

Wow, starting to get a little emotional. So let's just start the story so you can fall in love with these girls just like I did. Oh, by the way, it is infomercial time ... All of the girls' names have been changed as well as any identifying information to protect their privacy as well as some of the situations, diagnoses, and history.

Chapter 1
The beginning...

Now, where should I start? Well, let's start with the day that I will never forget. It was the first day in the group home.

After spending four weeks in training learning about how to deal with youth who are placed in a group home, learning different restraint techniques called Therapeutic Crisis Intervention (TCI), getting CPR-and-first-aid certified, and learning all the policies and procedures, I was finally allowed to go to the group home in which I was hired to work. Safe Haven hired me to be the clinical therapist in Group Home 6. As the clinical therapist, my responsibilities were to meet with all 10 of the girls twice a month for an hour, have group therapy once a week with them, and meet with any of the 10 girls when they were in crisis and wanted or needed to talk to me about something. So, now that you know why I was hired at Safe Haven, let's move on.

Oh yeah, remember what I was telling you earlier about different youth being placed in different group homes. Well, this is how Safe Haven is set up. Safe Haven has eight different group homes on its land of 120 acres (crazy, right, what I could do with that much land?). Group Homes 1 and 2 are where the boys stay. The boys who were 12 through 15 years old stayed in Home 1. The older boys 16 through 21 years old stayed in Home 2. Homes 3 and 4 were both SASY homes. The ratio in a SASY home is different because these youths have to be constantly monitored due to their predator-like nature. The ratio is 1:2 and 1:1 which means one staff to two youths or one staff to one youth. Home 3 was a boys' SASY Home and Home 4 was a girls' SASY Home. These homes only had about six to eight kids, and we really never saw the SASY youth (which was odd come to think about it). Homes 5 and 6 are where the girls stayed. Girls from 12 through 15 years old stayed in Home 5. The older girls 16 through 21 years old stayed in Home 6. Homes 7 and 8 are DD homes. Again, Home 7 is where the boys stayed and Home 8 is where the girls resided.

I worked in Group Home 6. The girls in this home called it the "Diva Home/House" because they all thought that they were bad ass bitches/DIVAs. On my first day in the home, I met Alyssa who was 16 years old at the time and African American. Alyssa was a truly beautiful girl with a beautiful personality at times. Alyssa always wore long shirts and long pants no matter how hot it was outside. As a matter of fact, it could be over 100 degrees out and she would be covered from head to toe. Why? Well, you will have to read my second book, *Group Home Drama: Alyssa's Story*, to find out the rationale behind Alyssa's attire. Sorry!

I met Lyla who was 17 years old and Kayla who was 15 years old and getting ready to turn 16 years old in two weeks. Lyla and Kayla were African-American sisters who had different fathers. Their personalities were like night and day. They were so different that you would not think that they were sisters if you saw them walking down the street. Did they have that sister rivalry going on? Of course, they did - not to mention that they didn't look like they were related. They have a juicy story filled with betrayal, lies, deception, and plenty of unfortunate bloodshed.

Marissa was a 17- year-old African American who was best friends with Lyla. I can truly say that her looks got her into a world of trouble all the time. Her looks got her into trouble so much that it was the main reason that she was at Safe Haven. I mean this girl is what grown men desired, not to mention that she had a "banging" body. When I tell you the stuff that Ms. Marissa went through you are going to swear up and down that I am lying.

Desiree was a 17-year-old African American who mostly stayed to herself. No one really liked her in the home because she acted like a child most of the time and was the least clean girl in the home. In fact, it was a fight everyday about her using the bathroom. On top of her having hygiene issues, Desiree also was diagnosed with bi-polar disorder and would flip the script several times a day. One minute she would be happy-go-lucky and the next minute she would be pissed off. After being pissed off, she would get/be depressed and then go back to her happy-go-lucky self. On top of all of that, do you know she had the audacity to get pregnant? This girl! Anyways, I will talk about Desiree and why she acted the way that she did in her book called "Desiree's Story."

Raven, the subject of this book, was an 18-year-old African American who loved to dress like a boy. She loved dressing like a boy so much that she cut off all her beautiful long hair so that she could look more like a boy. Because Raven wanted to dress and act like a boy, some of the girls or I should say the "girly girls" didn't want to be around her and tried several times to get her kicked out of the house. Raven was 5'1 and weighed around 110 pounds. She had an athletic body. Because of her physique, none of the girls ever really disrespected or messed with her. This is funny because you would think by her being so short people wouldn't be intimidated by her. But then, I thought the same thing and ... Well, you will find out soon enough after reading Raven's story.

Priscilla was the youngest in the home and was moved from Home 5 because she was jumped by all of the girls in that home. Priscilla was a 14-year-old African American who was a "pistol starter." The fact that she had to be moved into a home with girls who were older than her made her act even more like a badass than she really was. Priscilla was 5 feet tall and weighed about 98 pounds. She appeared to be an adorable girl. However, when she opened her mouth it was a totally different story.

Destiny was a 16-year-old African American who looked a lot older than she actually was. Most of the time, visitors thought that Destiny was one of the caregivers instead of one of the youths. Because of how old Destiny looked, she got into a lot of trouble - trouble that almost got her killed at one point in her life. Destiny was a troubled teen who had drug and alcohol problems because of everything that was happening in her life.

Tatiana and Zoey were both 18 years old, Hispanic, and stayed on the phone as much as they could. They were both family oriented. I know you're asking, "Well, if they are so family oriented why aren't they living with one of their family members?" (Well, you will have to read their books to find out. Sorry!)

The one thing that I can honestly say about all of these girls is that each one of them had strong, defined personalities. They acted and behaved certain ways as a survival mechanism. As onlookers, we tend to judge people who act and behave a certain way due to ignorance. Yes, I said ignorance. I used to prematurely judge people so harshly. But after working with these girls, getting to know them, and understanding their behaviors and personalities, it makes perfectly good sense as to why they did what they did and why they acted and treated others the way that they did.

Now, let me fill you in on a little secret that you need to know. When a new staff member starts working in any group home, the youth go through what is called a "Honey Moon" phase with that staff. Some of the youth act real nice. Some act like assholes. Some ignore the new staff all together because they are testing that staff. The youth really want to see what this staff is going to let them get away with. They want to know if that staff member is a push over, is afraid of them, is a drill sergeant, or if that staff member is trying to be their friend. Due to the fact that I have been working with youth for a very long time, for the first couple of weeks after I start a new job, all I do is watch, read, and listen. To break it down, I watch how the youth act and react to situations. I read their files, grievances, and any other important documentation. I also look at how they dress, how they clean, and how they keep their rooms, etc. Lastly, I listen to what the youth are saying. I learn what is important to them by the nature of their conversations and who they talk about and to whom they talk.

At Safe Haven, when you start, after you get out of training, you are shadowing another staff member for a few weeks so that you can learn the daily routine. For anyone who wants to work with youth or in a group home setting, the best advice that I can give you is this - be yourself and don't act like you are afraid of any youth (even if you are) because if you do that the youth will know and they will use it to their advantage. Don't get me wrong. If you are in fear that a youth might try to harm you, take the necessary steps to protect yourself. But if you meet a youth and you're afraid of them because of how they look or how big they are don't show them that you're scared of them. Do not try to be their friend (you're not there to be their friend). You are there to help them. Also, don't "bull-shit" them because they have been "bull-shitted" their whole lives and it will make them shut down on you.

It is important to maintain an appropriate, healthy relationship with the youth. If you follow these simple rules you will be fine. Oh yeah, I can't believe I almost forgot. Under no circumstances do you ever lie to a youth or promise them something that you do not know for a fact that you will be able to fulfill. These youths have been through enough and they don't need another person in their life who is going to lie to them and give them false hope.

The first few weeks of training are critical because not only are you learning the daily routine, learning the youth, and their behaviors, you are also learning the staff members with whom you will be working with and how they react to certain situations. This is very important to know because if you're not paying attention to how your team members react to certain situations you are setting yourself up to fail. What do I mean by this? Well, let me tell you. All situations are not this severe. With this being said, you have to develop a healthy, positive, trustworthy relationship with your fellow staff members or else you will have a lot of situations like the one I am about to tell you about.

Chapter 2

The situation...

At this point, I had been at Safe Haven for about a month. On this day, I just had walked into the home all happy-go lucky and ready to start my shift. As soon as I walked up to the door, I heard Raven (youth) and Susan, a staff member, arguing.

I thought to myself, "Damn, this is how I'm starting my afternoon? Really?" (Yeah, I worked the evening shift which was from 2:00 p.m. to 10:00 p.m.) Like a fool, I always arrived 30 to 45 minutes early for my shift. As I opened the door and Susan saw me, a look of relief came over her face and she decided that she wanted to walk out of the room and lock herself into the staff office.

By the way, Susan was not supposed to walk away from that youth in a crisis situation like this. Instead, Susan should have asked Raven if she was okay with talking to a different staff member. Mind you, I was the only staff on the floor at this time with 10 girls because Susan and Maria were in the office with the door locked looking at me and Raven through the window. Remember what I said about that ratio of 1:4 at all times. The third staff member, Thomas, was the floor supervisor, who was in the bathroom but quickly walked into the kitchen as the situation was unfolding and becoming hostile (which was a locked room as well). Like Susan, Thomas stared at Raven and me through the window.

All of the girls were sitting at the dining room table because it was homework time. Raven was standing in the living room and was refusing to sit down at the dining room table.

I asked Raven if she wanted to talk and she screamed and said, "No, the bitch I was talking to locked her scary ass in the staff office."

I asked Raven if she wanted to take a time out so that she could calm down.

Raven shook her head no and threw an orange at the staff office window. The windows were bullet proof so they didn't break.

I asked Raven to take a time out and she said, "No, fuck that" and threw another orange.

At this point, I called a Code Red which meant that all the girls had to go into their rooms and close their doors.

All of the girls went into their rooms. But of course, none of them actually closed their doors. While the girls were standing in their doorways, Raven continued to throw things everywhere. I felt like I was playing dodgeball as Raven threw oranges, chairs, books, and any and everything else that she could find. I know you're wondering if I was pissed off about this crisis situation that I was placed in. Hell yes, because my team was sitting and standing safely behind locked doors and left me in a crisis situation. Worst of all, I am in a situation that I didn't even start or should not have even been a part of. However, I got stuck cleaning up Susan's mess. The girls were standing in their doorways and could have gotten hit at any time. But, not one staff member came from behind their safely locked doors to do anything about it. Oh, are you asking why the girls would not close their doors?

Well, let me tell you, when you build a healthy rapport with the youth in the group home, they look out for you and will not allow anyone to hurt you, no matter if it's a staff member or another youth in the home. You have to remember that these youths don't have a lot of people in their lives who they can look up to and that they know truly cares about them. So when they find someone who cares about them and not a person that allows them to do whatever they want to do - a person who truly cares about them - they do everything in their power to protect that person.

Let me go back to the situation at hand. If I would have gotten hit by something that Raven was throwing towards me, the girls would have jumped her.

How do I know?

Because Lyla, Kayla, and Marissa were standing in their doorways yelling back and forth to each other, "Marissa, if something hits Ms. Lishay we gonna beat Raven's ass."

"Lyla, we sure are because the staff that is supposed to be out here with her don't give a fuck. They too scared to help Ms. Lishay."

So, at this time, I said a quick prayer (while I heard Lyla in the background saying, "Y'all scary ass staff need to get up off your asses and get out here now. Help her, you stupid bitches") and went into action because I had to de-escalate this situation quickly before it got worst.

In a group home, a minor situation can escalate into a deadly situation in a matter of seconds. Let's imagine for a minute if Raven would have thrown a chair at me and it accidently hit my leg. I would have fallen to the floor. The youth standing in their doorways would look at my face and see me hurt and in pain. Their heart rates would go into overdrive due to the pure excitement of the situation. Now they are acting on pure adrenaline due to their "flight or fright" response being triggered. Then three of the girls would have jumped Raven. Because Lyla, Kayla, and Marissa had a lot of respect from the other girls in the home, all of the other girls would have jumped in due to the fact that they didn't want to lose the respect of their fellow peers. The youth would have also jumped

Raven after seeing her hit a staff member whom the girls looked up to and respected. Now the girls are mad and go from jumping Raven to beating her with books and chairs and anything else she might have been throwing. Raven ends up in the hospital unconscious or in the morgue due to being hit, cut, or punched in the wrong place. All of the girls end up having federal charges on their records. The three ring leaders (as they will be called) or bullies end up with federal charges and incarcerated for 25 years to life and staff end up fired. This situation would have been a mess that could have happened in a matter of seconds - not minutes ... seconds.

So when I say this incident had to be resolved quickly I meant quickly because some of these girls "black out" when they start fighting. If those girls would have jumped Raven, there would not have been anything that I could have done but call the police and hope that they didn't kill Raven or beat her unconscious. (Please don't judge these girls.) You have to understand that it is extremely rare for them to find a person whom they know without a shadow of a doubt really, truly cares about them.

To me, to judge these girls would be to judge yourself because you are not going to let someone beat up and jump your child, your mother, or your best friend, are you? Are you? This group home setting is the only family that these youths know. To me, it's a shame that most of the staff who work at group homes or care facilities don't understand that. Now, back to the situation.

I looked at Raven and I started talking to her even though she was still throwing stuff. I know she is listening to me. How? Because the youths are always listening to what a staff member is saying. Mostly, because they are expecting staff to say the wrong thing, something dumb or something degrading to them so that they know without a shadow of doubt that they can't trust you and/or know that you really don't care about them.

So, I start talking to Raven in the third person, telling her that I care about her and that I know that she is not mad at me. I start telling her that she (Raven) has had a hard ass life and that I (Ms. Lishay) am so proud of her because she made it. (Remember what I said earlier about watching, looking, reading, and listening.) I took Raven back to that day when she was laying on the railroad tracks ready to give up, when a cop just so happened to drive by and pulled her off of the tracks before the train hit her and gave her a second chance at life.

I told her, I get it. You don't trust men because of the abuse you went through. And when you open up to a staff member it's hard and you just want us to listen. I get it, Raven. I swear to you I get it. I understand that after all of that, all you wanted to know is if Jesus loves you but instead of that you get a staff member who is trying to give you a bible lesson on how being gay is ungodly. That would upset me as well. (Now, I don't advise anyone to do or say what I am about to unless you know that child like the back of your hand because it can backfire on you.) At this point, I walked up to Raven and I saw the tears in her big brown eyes running down her cheeks. I hugged her and took the book out of her hand that she was about to throw.

I kept telling her I get it. I get it. I told her that I knew this had nothing to do with me and that I was not mad at her.

Truth be told, I wasn't mad at her because Raven has literally been through hell and back in the short time that she has been on this earth.

Raven had been through more in her 18 years in this world than most people have been through in their entire life. After that, Raven and I went for a walk and talked about what had just happened, how she felt about it, and what was going on inside her head now.

Raven apologized even though she didn't need to because I understood what was going on.

Raven told me that she thought Susan would be understanding and would talk to her about being gay and God not judging her and loving her for who she was. But instead, Susan got upset and told her that being gay was a sin and that God didn't love her and would never love her until she stopped acting gay.

Raven stated that Susan told her that she was going to burn in hell and that she should burn in hell because she could not understand how a woman would want to be with another woman and neither could God.

Raven then looked me in my eyes and asked me if what Susan said was true. Raven said, "You go to church and believe in God. Is it true? Is it?"

I looked at Raven and told her no that's not true. Jesus loves all of us. It is written that he died on the cross for our sins, not just Susan's sins or my sins, all of our sins. I also told her that all things work together for good to them that love God (Romans 8:28).

Raven and I walked back into the home and she went into her room and wrote in her journal that she allowed me to read sometimes. Even though I was not mad at Raven I was upset at the staff that left me in a crisis situation. We are supposed to work together as a team. There was no team on this day. On this day it was every man or woman for himself or herself.

Do you know that after the incident with Raven happened the staff had the audacity to talk to me and tried to tell me that I handled that situation very well. Now, I would like to think that I am a fairly nice person until you push me. But in my head I was thinking, "If you don't get the fuck away from me before I punch you in your fucking face." People who really know me say that they can tell what I am thinking by my expressions. Well, that day they must have known because after that, they didn't say anything to me. And that's the way I wanted it. I know you're probably thinking, "Well, how did that work"? From that day on, I kind of stayed to myself and focused on my job and attended to the needs and wants of the youth.

Well, it worked. Remember what I told you. I came in early that day. That was the day shift that I went through that ordeal with. I worked mainly with the night shift because I enjoyed working with that staff. Those hours worked for me because I did other stuff during the day. I worked out and volunteered at my church mentoring inner-city youth in that neighborhood. That neighborhood, by the way, is one of the roughest neighborhoods in the city. A lot of these kids' family members had gotten shot and killed by other kids in the neighborhood. Let's get back to Raven ...

Chapter 3
Raven who?

That night, Raven came out and showed me her journal. She wanted me to read some of it. At this point, I am going to allow Raven to tell you about herself through her journal writings.

The early journals ...

Hey everyone. My name is Raven and I am an African-American female who is now 18 years old. I am 5'1" and weigh 110 pounds. I grew up in Englewood. My mother was a prostitute and would allow her male clients to sleep with me when they didn't want her or they wanted someone younger. My mother started making me sleep with grown men when I turned 8 years old. I have been asked by different workers how can I remember what happened to me when I was 8 years old and I just want to slap them. If it was a traumatic experience, of course, I'm not going to forget it. At least that's what Ms. Lishay told me.

I was in my room playing with the only two Barbie dolls I had. I knew when it was time because my mother would put in one of those Walt Disney movies (to this day, I still can't watch one of those movies because I freak out.) then she would give me a shot that I found out was heroin. The man would come into the room and start touching my hair and undoing whatever hair style I had. He would then start touching my chest and my back and telling me that he was a nice guy and that he just wanted to play a game. He would make me get up and dance to the music coming from the movie that my mother put in. Then he would tell me to sit down on the bed next to him and start touching my private spots and he would tell me to put his penis in my mouth. He would then lay me down and go inside my private spots. I was dizzy and light headed but I screamed because of how painful it was. He would put his hand over my mouth and tell me to shut the fuck up and tell me to tell him that I loved him.

After it was over he told my mother that she had a good one and that she needed to check on me because he broke my cherry really good. I did not know what that meant at the time but I was relieved that it was over. My mother would always put me in the bathtub afterwards and would tell me to say that my period started if I started to bleed at school. She told me that if I said anything different that bad people would come kill her (my mother) and take me to a place where I would have to do this to a man every hour. I was so scared that the teacher would catch me in a lie so I started telling my teachers to ask my mother what happened and that I didn't feel well. The first time it happened to me I thought I was going to die. It was so painful and I was bleeding for a week. I always wondered to myself if I told my teacher what would have really happened. Would my teacher have taken me in? Would what my mom told me really happen? Or would they think I was lying because I wanted some kind of attention or something.

After the 12th time, I stopped counting. I stopped caring. I stopped feeling. My mother would always tell me that I was ugly and that I was not going to be nothing but a two-dollar hoe. I don't really remember my father. When I asked my mother, she would always say it didn't matter because he didn't want me, love me, and didn't give a shit about me. At the age of 10 years, I went to the hospital and had a pap smear done due to the constant bleeding, pain, and itching in my vaginal area. Two weeks later I was told that I had an incurable STD and four other

STDs that I could get rid of. I was told that because of the severity of one of the STDs and it going untreated for so long and the damage that had been done to my cervix, that I would not be able to have kids. The next day, I walked to the railroad tracks and tied my legs to them and lied across them. I was so scared but so happy at the same time when I heard the train coming. I thought to myself, "God it's finally about to be over." God, I finally will be able to meet you and ask you why I had to go through all of this." I thought finally some answers as to why I had to suffer my entire life. Well, I can't say my entire life. Everything was fine when I was a baby up until my dad left my mom and she started prostituting herself to keep her apartment. But the end was near. The train started blowing its horn, the tracks started to rattle and shake, and the lights were so bright, I thought the light was coming to me. Then I started to hear a muffled sound to my right. It was getting closer and closer, and then I heard a voice.

It was a police officer yelling, telling me to get up.

I thought to myself there is no fucking way that this is happening to me right now. Why me? Just turn around and let me die.

The police officer ran up to me and started untying the rope I used to tie my legs down with.

I got angry and I started hitting, punching, and kicking him as I was yelling at him to go away. I yelled at him to just leave me alone and go away with every hit. I yelled and cried and hit him again. God, just let me die.

The police officer pulled me up right before the train passed us by. I had so many tears in my eyes that I couldn't even see the cop or the train. The police officer took me to the hospital and I was placed into the care of child protective services. My first placement was at some married couple's foster home. I did everything I could to get out of there because the woman's husband kept looking at me like I was a piece of meat and made me feel uncomfortable. He would come into my room at night and sit on the edge of my bed asking me questions about my past. My mother came to see me once while I was staying there before she died from AIDS. I have been in the care of child protective services since I was 10 years old. Before being placed in this group home called Safe Haven I was placed in three different foster care homes.

    The second foster home I was in was in the suburbs with an old lady. She had five other foster kids in her home and I didn't like any of them. We constantly fought because they kept stealing my stuff. One night I heard one of the foster kids in my room looking in my book bag. The kid was trying to steal the necklace that I was told my dad had bought for me. I ran into the kitchen, got a knife, and went after the girl. I was SASS'ed (which stands for Screening, Assessment, and Support Services) that night and stayed in the psych ward for a month. I didn't care because all I cared about at the time was the fact that I got my necklace back. (SASS is a crisis mental health service program for children and adolescents who are experiencing a psychiatric emergency.) The foster parents can call the cares line at any time if they feel like a youth may need hospitalization or community-based mental health care.

After the third foster home placement didn't work out I guess child protective services said we will never find a foster care home that she will do well in. I have been at Safe Haven since I was 12 years old. So I guess this is home. It's not so bad. I get to meet different people a lot because the staff members don't stay that long.

The way my life started out is totally different from how it is now. When my mother died a worker came to the group home and gave me some of my mother's belongings. There was a huge photo album in her things. When I opened it I smelled my mother's perfume and saw a picture of my mom and dad standing in front of their home. I was told that my mom and dad used to live in Oak Park, Illinois. I saw pictures of me in front of a Christmas tree that had a lot of gifts under it. I couldn't understand what happened. We looked so happy.

What happened? I asked the worker about my father and she asked me if my mom ever told me anything about my dad.

To that I responded no by shaking my head.

The worker informed me that my father passed away when I was 6 years old. He was a lawyer - the kind that dealt with criminals and putting them away. The worker said that he died from cancer.

The worker also told me that my mom was a stay-at-home mom and was pregnant when my dad passed away.

I asked the worker what happened to my brother or sister.

The worker put her head down, apologized, and stated that my mom lost the baby and was hospitalized for a while after that. After she got out of the hospital she got hooked on drugs, ran through my dad's savings, and couldn't afford the house. That's how we ended up in Englewood and that is why she became a prostitute.

The worker asked me if I had any more questions and I told her no.

She then asked me if I ever wanted to talk to some family members on my father's side to give her a call as she handed me her business card.

I put the card in the back of the photo album and put the photo album under my bed.

As of now, I still have only seen the pictures on those first three pages in that photo album. I can't bring myself to open it again. I always thought that my dad was a drug dealer or a pimp or that my mom didn't know who he was. But to hear that my father was a good guy who appeared to love me up until the day he died, I don't know … I just don't know …

How am I supposed to feel about this? How am I supposed to deal with this? I don't know. Why did he have to die?

What did he do that was so bad that God said, "You're not going to see your daughter grow up."

Why wasn't my mother stronger? What did I do that made her give up on life? What the fuck did I do to make her look at me and say, "This little bitch is going to make me some money with her ugly ass." What? Why?

I ended up getting addicted to heroin because of my mother. She would give it to me before she sent a man in my room to sleep with me.

(At the bottom of the page of Raven's journal, she drew a picture of her, her mother, and her father holding a baby. By the way, Raven was an excellent artist. But she drew an X on the picture of her father holding the baby with a red pen. The pages were hard and some of the ink had been smeared like Raven was crying and her tear drops had fallen on different spots of the page.)

Raven came into my office a few weeks later and gave me a journal that I had never seen before. She informed me that she started writing in this journal a few weeks after I came to Safe Haven. Raven was holding the journal so tight in her hand that it was starting to bend in the middle.

Raven started shaking and said, "Ms. Lishay, please don't judge me after you read this." I don't know why I started doing it but now I can't stop and I think I might need to go see a doctor."

I raised my hand to take the journal and Raven jerked, stepped back and said, "You're not going to judge me, are you?"

As I looked up from the journal I noticed that Raven had tears in her eyes.

I asked Raven to sit down for a minute.

I walked over to my door, closed it, and sat down in front of her so that we were face to face.

I asked Raven, "Why do you think I am going to judge you?"

Raven responded by saying, "People always tell me if something appears to be too good most likely it is."

I asked her to elaborate. Raven then said, "Well, you always tell us that you don't judge us and that you have no right to judge us because you can be judged in the very same way. Most of the time when people look at me they have already judged me just from the way I look and ... and ... I know it's wrong but I judge people and ... and …. I know after you read this, that there is no way that you are not going to be able to judge me."

I asked Raven, "How could you think that? You know that there is nothing that you can do that will make me judge you. I might get upset or not understand but judge …. judge … Raven, you know that's not me. Do you want to talk about what you wrote in the journal first? Or do you want me to read it and then we talk about it? It's up to you.

Raven was sitting on the couch with her legs crossed. She looked down at the journal, picked it up, and handed it to me.

I reached out to take it, and she held on to it for six seconds before she let it go. I asked her if she wanted me to read it now.

Raven said, "Yes. Can I stay here while you read it?"

I told Raven, of course, she could. I told Raven she could stay in the room while I read it but I knew that she was going to be looking at my facial expressions and trying to read my body language as I read through it. I was hoping and praying that I could control my body language and facial expressions while I was reading through the journal. Raven was really good at picking up on a person's negative expressions or negative body movements. That would be another conversation that I would have to have with her.

So, I told Raven that I was about to start reading her journal and that she could tell me to stop at any time if she started to feel uncomfortable.

Raven said okay.

I went back to my desk and placed the journal on the table. As I opened the journal to the first page I could see Raven out the corner of my eye. She had her legs crossed. She started biting her nails and began to rock back and forth as she was staring me in the face. I started reading what she wrote and had to focus on maintaining the proper body language and facial expressions.

Raven had written in the journal that she wanted to know what it felt like to be a man because she did not understand them. Raven stated that she was in school one day and saw one of the boys grab himself. Raven went into the bathroom and grabbed herself in the same area. Raven then had the urge to urinate so she went into the bathroom stall and pulled her pants all the way down and tried to pee like a boy would. Raven started to pee but was getting her underwear wet. Raven stopped peeing and remembered that she had a pen in her pocket. Raven took the pen apart and held the outer tube between her fingers.

Raven then started to wonder if she could fit the tube opening into her urethra. Raven inserted it into her urethra and started peeing. Raven stated that she was surprised that it was working and that she could aim her urine wherever she wanted it to go. She stated that the first time she did it, it hurt really bad because the pen tube opening was too big. Raven said that when she went school supply shopping she bought pens with smaller tube openings. Raven also wrote that since she started inserting, she has not been able to stop and that she inserts every time she has to go to the bathroom now.

After reading what Raven wrote in the journal, I closed it and asked her how she felt about me reading what she had written and what she has been doing.

Raven shrugged her shoulders and said that she didn't know. She said that she was relieved that I knew because she was experiencing a lot of pain down there and that it hurt really badly when she inserts now and sits down.

Raven asked me how I felt about what she has been doing.

I told her that I am glad that she trusted me enough to tell me that she has been doing something that has been causing her a lot of pain. I also informed her that one of the staff that works on the second shift will be taking her to the emergency room today when they come in.

I asked her if she had a certain staff member that she wanted to take her and she stated that she wanted Tasha to take her.

I asked Raven how long had she been inserting and she stated that she started inserting after she saw that boy grab himself.

I asked her again, when she started inserting and she said, "I'm telling the truth. It was after I saw that boy grab himself."

I looked at Raven and didn't say anything for about 20 seconds and then she said, "Ok, ok. Damn it, Ms. Lishay. It was after I saw that boy grab himself but it was when the worker came up here and gave me that crap that belonged to my mother."

I said, "Ok I believe you."

She stated, "Yeah, I bet you do. I don't know. I just wanted to know what it felt like to be a man and understand why they act the way they do. I guess. Fuck, I don't know. I'm fucked up in the head, right?"

I told Raven, "Stop talking like that. Pause the critical tape, Raven."

Raven stated, "I can't Ms. Lishay. I don't understand or know why I started doing it."

I then said, "Raven, you have been through stuff in your life that the strongest person in the world would find hard to deal with. Raven, I have told you that there is no such thing as a "normal person." We are all abnormal and do stuff that other people don't understand."

Raven then replied by saying, "I guess, but I think something is stuck inside because of how much pain I'm in."

When Tasha arrived that evening, I called her into my office and asked if she could take Raven to the emergency room.

Tasha said, "Of course, but why?"

Raven and I explained to her what was going on. Raven did not return that night due to the fact that she had to be operated on. A thin plastic part of the pen had broken off and got stuck far up in her urethra and they had to operate on her to get it out. She was extremely sore for weeks and admitted that she had tried to insert a few times after the operation. After months of being in therapy, Raven finally stopped inserting. I later learned that another girl in the group home had started inserting all kinds of things like Raven. But this is about Raven.

Let's get back to Raven's journal ….

Chapter 4

This is staff?

Some of the staff members here really care about us. However, it's more staff here that don't give a fuck about us. And they show us every damn day. The staff that care about us they (management) get rid of. When it comes to actually having healthy relationships like the management tell the staff to have with us, it does not happen because no one wants to talk to a staff that they know don't give a damn about them. I think it's a jealously thing.

Just like the fact that there is not one black director here but 90 percent of the kids here are fucking black. How does that make any kind of sense? So you're telling me that there is not one black person here qualified to be a director?

The funny thing is that Safe Haven thinks that the kids here are dumb and don't see what is going on. Why is there a white person always directing the black people? Is this the way life really is? This seems like slavery. If Safe Haven is really here to help us, why is there not more staff here that we can relate to? Now, Lord knows I don't have anything against white people but as a black kid I want to see that some of my own people have made it. That's why I don't watch television because it's all fake. I never see a black family doing well and having or dealing with normal everyday-type drama. Every time you see black people on television it's about drugs, sex, and money. Really? Is that what every other nationality really thinks that we are about or care about?

    They hire all these white people to care for us. I don't understand how the fuck a white person is supposed to help me. They don't know what it's like to be black, live in poverty, and be in constant fear because the bedtime stories I go to sleep to are gunfire and voices screaming for help. Most of them act like they are scared of us. How are you gonna be scared of us and work with us? Stupid. Who created this? If black people were raising white kids, white people would have something to say about it. I promise you that. They don't give a fuck about us. They even tell us they don't give a fuck about us and that we are just a check for them until they find something better.

It's so crazy because every time we get a white kid in here the staff treats them like they are more important than anyone else in the home. Their Court Appointed Special Advocate (CASA) workers go to bat for them as well as their attorneys. It's like they can do no wrong. The fucked up thing is that they are always the first ones to leave this place and be placed in a permanent foster home. That's why some of these staff members get jumped. I can't lie. I look forward to those days because those are the only times when we get true fucking justice. It's justice for the staff beating us when they are supposed to be restraining us. It's justice from them calling us stupid bitches who will never be anything or bitches who stink and are too dumb to know how to take care of themselves. So, all the girls get together and decide who we had enough of and we jump they ass. They always quit. It's so funny. They deserve it. Now they can go get that job they really want. Hey, we are only helping them out. (Ms. Lishay: I know you are thinking to yourself these kids are just mean and evil. But what I have to say to that is, "don't judge a book by its cover.").

Believe me before we jump staff we try to go about it the right way (the so-called chain of command) but no one listens to us or believes us. We file grievances and no one ever gets back to us on them. Remember what I told you earlier about the staff who actually care about us and how Safe Haven gets rid of them. The only time our grievances are investigated is when management is trying to get rid of these staff members. So, you tell me what would you do if you did everything by the book and nothing happens?

It's not right, but it's also not right for staff to treat us like shit because they can or because they had a bad day and want to take that shit out on us. All we want is to be treated like human beings, not animals. You would think that the staff at this place would be understanding and really here ready to help us. But no, everyone is out for himself or herself.

Most of the time when staff members come to work they are gossiping about another staff they don't like. But they tell us that we act like dumb ass kids. Who comes to work to gossip and tries to get another staff fired because that staff actually does their job? Just fucking stupid!

Chapter 5

The Raid...

Today at school during lunch a bunch of us got together and starting talking about this mean white male staff member named Tom that they hired. Tom is the one who likes to joke about keeping us niggas in check with his friends while he is in the staff office thinking that no one can hear him. Us kids have filed over 20 grievances on him. Can you believe that he has even been caught on tape saying, "These niggas ain't shit! That's why we here man, to fuck these little niggas up. They have tried to file grievances on me but my supervisor has a crush on me so nothing is going to happen. I be in here whooping these niggas' asses" and nothing has happened. How is that fair? So when we hear Tom saying this shit, what? We just supposed to act like the shit was never said? Oh, hell no.

We also started talking about this bitch named Mary that they hired that acts like she is better than everyone. She was flinging her long, blond hair in people's faces after she made some smart ass remark to them. She also has a habit of telling on everyone. She can come in here and wash her hair every night and bring and sit a television on the floor when she works overnight. She is supposed to be checking our rooms every 15 minutes, but instead she talks on her phone when no other staff can. How is this shit fair? We have filed multiple grievances on her as well and nothing has happened. One night, one of the girls got tired of Mary getting away with stuff and decided that she was going to wait until all of her peers were asleep (because that's when Mary would go out to her car and grab her television) and Mary went outside. It would always take Mary 10 minutes to bring the television in because she would always have a smoke while she was outside and let me tell you, she was not always just smoking cigarettes. So while Mary was outside smoking, the girl took a picture of the clock, the hall that Mary was supposed to be sitting in, and a picture of Mary walking back inside with the television in her arms. It was the perfect shot because the clock was right above the doorway. However, when Mary saw the girl out of her room she sat the television down by the door and ran into the girl's room. However, the girl had hidden the camera in her room.

Mary screamed at the girl, "Give me that got damn camera now, you little bitch."

The girl told her that she owned that camera and that she was not giving her anything.

Mary then pushed the girl and called for a restraint. But she made damn sure she took that television back outside before any staff came to help her with the restraint. Mary lied and told the other staff that the girl had a weapon in her room and the staff tore the room apart while the other staff had the girl in a restraint.

We all felt bad for the girl because Mary found the camera and told the girl, "Now clean this shit up! You heard me! Clean this shit up now!"

Mary broke the camera, took the film out of it (exposed the film to light), and gave the girl the camera back. When the supervisor came in, the girl told her what happened but the supervisor didn't take her seriously and believed what Mary had told her. Worst of all, the supervisor would not replace the camera that Mary broke because Mary told the supervisor that the girl dropped the camera and then told her that she was going to lie on Mary and say that she did it.

We also talked about this staff member named Tiffany who allowed one of the kid's roommates to beat the other kid up after she fell asleep. The girl punched her roommate in the face and the stomach while she was asleep to the point where the girl had to be hospitalized. There was no investigation or anything. So because the director and the CEO were allowing this stuff to continue we had to take this crap into our own hands. So we put one kid in charge of this raid. We gave this kid the days that our favorite staff worked so that she can let us know what day and time we would do this on.

The thing about a raid is that all available staff gets called to help restrain and we don't like involving the staff that we know care about us in this type of thing. So we decided to do this on a Monday in the evening. There will always be staff working that we don't want involved so we have certain peers take them somewhere. For example, we might go clothes shopping or to the library, etc. so that they won't be involved. We had everything planned. The way it was going to start was by getting Priscilla to start an argument with Mary. It was always so easy to pull Mary into an argument in which she would be calling the kid a bitch in a matter of minutes. Priscilla was down for whatever because she hated Mary and how she treated others.

It was almost time to get everything kicked off when we heard Desiree and Mary arguing. Desiree was walking by the staff office when she heard Mary talking to another staff member about her. According to Desiree, Mary was saying that she could not stand Desiree and that she was a nasty ass bitch and that any guy who wanted to have sex with her was a damn fool and would end up catching a STD from her. All we heard was Mary telling Desiree that she needed to mind her own damn business and that if she was offended by hearing the truth about herself that she needed to get her stinking ass in the shower.

When Desiree heard Mary say that, it was over. It was like Desiree checked out and was taken over by the devil himself. Mary was shaking her hair and she made the mistake of doing it a little too close to Desiree. Desiree grabbed Mary's hair, twisted her hand in her hair (Mary went airborne for a few seconds), and Desiree threw Mary across the room and started punching her in the face. Staff called a Code Red and it took five staff members to get Desiree off of Mary. But it was too late. It was going down. Once the kids heard that Code Red they knew it was time. All of us started attacking staff members with any and everything we could find. We had forks, bats, fire extinguishers, chairs, books, and anything else that was in sight that we could use as a weapon.

While I was getting restrained, Lyla had printed out over 500 copies of all the grievances that we had filed and started throwing them all over the place. She put them in all the staff boxes, in the CEO's office, and anywhere else that staff would look. It was so much blood everywhere. There were about eight different staff members who had been knocked unconscious, including Mary and Tom. Things had gotten so out of hand that one of the kids had called the police. Over 50 kids got arrested that night and the rest of us were placed on lock down.

When the overnight shift started, things were just starting to settle down. The overnight crew didn't get any sleep that night because they were up cleaning and talking to the kids about what happened. All of us felt bad about how bad things got but we were tired. We were tired of being treated like crap and tired of being used and abused. I thought the point of us coming to the group home was for us to stop being abused mentally, physically, and spiritually. Yes, I said spiritually. I don't understand how a person can want to help someone but don't have any kind of spiritual relationship. Don't get me wrong, because I can't stand staff that is always forcing Jesus down your throat but act like demons. I don't understand how people like that can even be hired. They come in here and tell us that we can't talk about Jesus or anything spiritual. I'm not saying that there are not kids here who don't believe that there is a God because there are.

What I am saying is that if we do have spiritual beliefs we should be able to talk about it and practice our beliefs. Things are so messed up. A few of the non-believers who yelled at us and told us that they didn't want us talking about God or our spiritual beliefs were among the staff that got knocked unconscious. I don't think the CEO and some of these staff get it. We are supposed to be getting help here. I can't wait until we have group therapy later today.

Chapter 6

Therapy time...

It was later today and time for the second shift to start. Ms. Lishay was pissed after coming in. She already knew about everything that had happened. All of the kids went into the group therapy room and waited. Five minutes had passed by and Ms. Lishay still had not walked into the room yet. Ms. Lishay was never late for therapy (as a matter of fact, Ms. Lishay was never late for anything). I asked staff if I could go to my room to get my notebook because my room is on the other side of her office and I wanted to see what was taking her so long.

As I walked by Ms. Lishay's door, I saw her sitting in her chair with her head down and her hands in a prayer position. She looked up at me and her eyes had a shine to them like she had tears in her eyes. I walked into my room, grabbed a notebook, and walked my ass back past her office with my head down. I could tell that she was disappointed in us. It was 10 minutes later before Ms. Lishay had walked into the group therapy room. The look of disappointment on her face made several of us kids break down to the point of tears. It was always different with Ms. Lishay because we knew she cared about all of us. I mean she really cared about all of us. Ms. Lishay asked all of the staff to leave the room. A couple of the staff members had gotten upset but they knew that Ms. Lishay was in charge when the director was not present so they had to leave. There was a huge oversized window so that staff could look into the room. So most of them just sat by the window and watched us.

Ms. Lishay closed the door, sat down, and was silent. Kayla raised her hand to ask a question and Ms. Lishay told her to put her hand down. It's like Kayla raising her hand pissed her off even more. Ms. Lishay then said, "I know damn well you guys don't want to talk now after all that shit that you guys just pulled last night." She then asked us what we were thinking and how long did we have this planned out because she knew that all of the group home kids would have not joined in if it was not planned.

Priscilla raised her hand. And when Ms. Lishay looked at her she said, "Ms. Lishay, we are sorry! We are tired. Staff here is not like you and Tasha. They don't give a fuck about us."

Ms. Lishay then bit her lip and said, "How many times do I have to tell you that not everyone is going to like you. Not everyone is gonna care about you or give you the time of day." Unfortunately, this is the kind of world we live in."

Lyla asked why did Ms. Lishay and Tasha care about us.

Ms. Lishay said, "Because some of us look at our job as a calling and know that people should not be judged because of their situation, color, sex, background, or whatever else people judge one another on. I keep telling you guys no one is better than another person. People want to believe that because they are rich or famous or whatever that they are better than others but they are not. What do I always tell you guys? We could be on the same plane as these famous rappers and actors that you guys love so much or even the richest man or woman in the world but when that plane starts to go down to crash we are all going to die together. No special plane or jet is gonna come out of nowhere and get them off of that plane before it crashes."

    Ms. Lishay went on to say that "I believe that God created all of us equal and the same. The world is like this because of mankind. Mankind decided to put us in this asinine ranking order. Mankind created slavery. Mankind is destroying this world. Until we get it in our heads that we have to work together in order to survive before we completely destroy this planet this is how things are going to be. Like I keep telling you guys you can do whatever you want to do in this life. The only reason that you won't accomplish your goal is because you gave up."

I raised my hand and asked Ms. Lishay how do we deal with staff talking about us and beating us up when they are supposed to be restraining us? How do we deal with the white staff here that judge us and treat us like we will always be beneath them?

Desiree chimed in and said that all of the white staff members are not bad.

I then stated that I knew that and that John, the white therapist in Home 2, was cool as hell. All the other kids started shaking their heads in agreement and saying yeah that's true.

Ms. Lishay responded by saying, "That we were not always going to be here in this group home." She then apologized for the unjust way that we have been treated by staff here and told us that we have to be strong. Ms. Lishay told us again that her door was always open and that we could talk to her whenever we needed to. After that, Ms. Lishay appeared to be a little calmer and looked less disappointed in us. She was still clearly mad at what we had done but we were using our words like she always asked us to do.

Ms. Lishay was well-respected by the kids at Safe Haven because of how she treated us. I mean she actually listened to us and went out of her way to help us accomplish whatever goal we were trying to achieve at that time. She was not perfect though and might get mad that I am saying this. Like I said she always listened to us but one day she came in and you could tell that she was forcing herself to stay awake. She looked like she was in a lot of pain as well.

Anyways, long story short, she had a therapy session with Desiree and Desiree had walked out looking all sad. We asked her what happened and she said, "I must have been complaining too much because Ms. Lishay started to fall asleep on me." Ms. Lishay apologized to Desiree but it was funny because Ms. Lishay did what all of us wanted to do when Desiree started complaining. But Ms. Lishay went to our court dates with us as well as our reviews and advocated for us. Not only was she respected by the kids here but a lot of staff would confide in her and would try to have therapy sessions with her even though they knew they were supposed to call that 800 number that was given to them when they first started. No matter if a staff was trying to talk with Ms. Lishay about a problem they were having, she always put us first. We would walk in and she would tell the staff to come back. It's so funny because the staff would be all mad but we appreciated it because she didn't act like she was better than us.

We talked about different ways we could have handled certain situations that led up to the raid. Even though we did not want to admit it, Ms. Lishay was right. But she never threw anything up in our face or judged us and that's why even when she called us out on our shit or yelled at us, we respected her because we knew she was doing it out of love - love. Wow! I really believe that she loves all of us. I mean she would have to, right, in order to want the best for us? Wow, this takes me back to that horrible church experience that I had. Oh my God! I remember it like it was yesterday. I wanted to fight the pastor I was so mad, lol.

Chapter 7

The church experience...

So, about three months after Ms. Lishay started, I decided that I wanted to join a church. Some of the kids had been going to this local church and were talking about all the cool stuff they were doing and how the pastor was really nice and that they loved going to this church. It wasn't the kind of church I was used to going to but I thought to myself if they all like it maybe I will, too. So that Sunday when Tasha came around and asked who all was going to church that day I told her that I was going, too. Tasha was so happy because she had been trying to get me to go to church with them for the longest.

The church service was not bad at all and I really enjoyed the pastor's message. After service, Lyla asked me to come with her so that I could meet the pastor so I said ok. Lyla introduced me to the pastor and we started to talk as Lyla walked off. The pastor started asking me your typical church questions like "Am I saved? Have I been to church before? What church was I going to before? Then he asked me why I stopped attending church. This is where everything went left. I told him about the stuff that I had been through when I was growing up and that I was a lesbian. The pastor's eyes got wide and he started talking about how being a lesbian was a sin.

I became really upset because I did not think that out of all people I would be judged by a pastor. The pastor and I started arguing. Tasha heard us and ran up to find out what was going on. After the pastor told her what happened Tasha grabbed me, gave me a hug, apologized, and we left. When we got into the van I started crying because I didn't understand why a pastor would judge me. I didn't ask to be like this. I didn't ask for my life to be like this. I didn't ask for none of this shit. If it wasn't for that stupid cop I wouldn't even be here. Sometimes I feel like God kept me here so that I would be miserable. I feel like I am only here to suffer.

What's wrong with me? What the hell is wrong with me? Wow, this is taking me right back to the way I was feeling then. When we got back to the home, I went to Ms. Lishay's office and sat down.

Ms. Lishay asked me if I was okay.

I didn't say anything.

Ms. Lishay asked me if she should talk to Tasha and I shook my head no.

Ms. Lishay then asked me if something happened at the church.

I shook my head yes.

Ms. Lishay then said that she was not a mind reader and that if I wanted her to help me that I would have to open up that mouth of mine.

So I told her what had happened and she started laughing.

I didn't think anything was funny and thought that she had lost it until she explained to me why she was laughing.

Ms. Lishay stated that she was not laughing at me and that she was laughing at the situation.

Ms. Lishay asked me, "What did I expect to happen?"

She said the kind of church that we went to was very old school and very strict. She explained how in that church (according to that pastor) none of us would ever make it to heaven. Ms. Lishay then explained how we are all sinners and how Jesus died on the cross for all of us. We had a nice spiritual conversation and then she handed me a card with the name of a church on it and told me that we could go there on Tuesday for their weekday service.

I told Ms. Lishay that I was done with the church thing, and she told me that I wasn't.

Ms. Lishay reminded me of the day we met and how I didn't want to open up to her because of how I hated the therapist before her and thought that therapy was a waste of time.

Ms. Lishay told me that every therapist is different and that you have to shop around until you find the right one. Ms. Lishay also told me that some therapists shouldn't even be therapists because they are not good at all and don't care about people.

I remember she told me the story about one of her friends going to a therapist who fell asleep during the session and how her friend had to shake him to wake him up and how her friend felt like me and didn't want to go to another therapist after that. What I can say about Ms. Lishay is that she never actually fell asleep on any of us. She might have started to but she never actually fell completely asleep. Plus, I feel like she was kind of justified with that Desiree situation. Ms. Lishay always tells us to stop complaining and to work on fixing the problem instead. To this day, I don't know if Ms. Lishay did that on purpose to Desiree or if she was really tired because no joke, she really looked like she was in pain but she was not the type of person who was going to come right out and tell you. Anyways, back to the story...

It was now Tuesday and I was dreading it. I knew Ms. Lishay wouldn't make me go somewhere just to be hurt all over again intentionally. But what if these people were the same way?

Ms. Lishay came to my room and said that it was time to go. I decided that I was really going to dress like a dude on this day because if I was going to be insulted again at least I was going to be comfortable.

Ms. Lishay asked me if that was what I was wearing.

I said, "Yes, why you don't like it?"

Ms. Lishay laughed and said come on girl it's time to go.

Ms. Lishay and I got in the van and drove to the church. Ms. Lishay laughed at me as we were pulling up to the church and said, "Come on scary cat." Ms. Lishay has never been a back row sitter and made me sit in the fourth row. The service was going well, but in my head I was thinking that the other service was good, too. I started looking around at the people and they appeared to be nice and smiled when they looked at me. The service was coming to an end and all I wanted to do was run out but Ms. Lishay grabbed my arm and said let's go meet the preacher.

As we walked up to the preacher my stomach dropped and my mouth was extremely dry. The preacher started asking me questions and I was like here we go again. The preacher then told me that I didn't have to be afraid and to be myself because he accepted me for who I was and then he introduced me to his boyfriend. My mouth dropped and I wanted to hit Ms. Lishay for allowing me to feel so anxious when she knew the whole time that I would love this church.

Long story short, I ended up signing up for their Gay and Lesbian Support Group. This group has helped me out a lot and has allowed me to accept myself just the way that I am. I have become friends with a lot of kids in the support group and love going to group and church during the week. It's like I have my very own thing that I do without my peers. It's like it's mine - my time to be without them. Don't get me wrong. I like the peers that I live with in this group home, but I guess it's like a family where sometimes you just want to have something to yourself.

Chapter 8

My first real kiss…..

One night during our Gay and Lesbian Support Group, this girl walked in. She had long curly hair. She was around my height. She looked biracial. You could tell that she was shy. Her name was Lilly. All of us welcomed her into the group. A few weeks later, she started to open up and talk about her experiences with being a lesbian. A few weeks after that, we started talking and became friends. When I met with Ms. Lishay for our weekly one-on-one session I told her about how me and Lilly were becoming friends and how I started having feelings for her.

Ms. Lishay asked me if Lilly had the same feelings that I had.

I told Ms. Lishay that I didn't know but that I wanted her to be my girlfriend.

Ms. Lishay informed me that I had to find out how Lilly felt about me and if she was even ready to start dating because of the stuff that I had told Ms. Lishay Lilly had been through.

I said, "Fine, the next time I go to group I am going to talk to her about it."

During our next group meeting, I pulled Lilly to the side and asked her if she has a girlfriend. Lilly said that she didn't and that after all the stuff she had been through she was not ready to start dating again until now. Lilly then asked me if I was seeing someone.

I told her no, I haven't found anyone that I wanted to date and that the kids at the group home I lived with were more like family to me.

Lilly then asked me if there was anyone in our group that she would want to date and I got really nervous. But all the while I'm thinking to myself, play it cool, stay cool, and just tell her.

I told her no, not until she came along.

Lilly smiled and said okay that's good.

From that night on we were good. We started talking all the time and writing each other letters, especially when I got into trouble and couldn't talk on the phone. I really enjoyed reading her letters because they were like poems. Her letters always smelled good like the perfume she wears all the time.

One night, the Gay and Lesbian Support Group went on an outing to the 69 Roller Rink. It was the best night of my life. Lilly and I skated while we were holding hands the whole night. We shared a chocolate milkshake and cheese fries. We started talking more about our past, how we have overcome it, and the people who have helped us along the way.

I told Lilly about Ms. Lishay and Tasha and how they have helped me so much.

I told her how Ms. Lishay and Tasha really care about us and that staff like them are extremely rare at Safe Haven.

Lilly asked me if I had to attend therapy or if I was going because I wanted to.

I told her that we don't have an option and that therapy was a part of our program. I told her that before Ms. Lishay started, all of the girls hated going to therapy because that therapist didn't care about us and how we were glad when she left.

It was almost time for us to leave and Lilly and I hugged each other.

Lilly then made eye contact with me and French-kissed me. Lilly's kiss was everything that I thought it would be and more.

    From that day on, all I could think about was the next time I would see Lilly - the next time I would get to hug her and kiss her. Lilly was everything that I could possibly want in a girlfriend. For once in my life I felt like everything was going to be okay. I felt like I had a reason to live and that I could actually be happy like Ms. Lishay had been telling me I could be. My whole life I felt like I have been struggling just to keep my head above water. Things were finally changing and I feel like I'm floating in the water now.

Chapter 9

The New Girl...

Remember the girl I told you about who took a picture of Mary with her camera and Mary broke her phone and didn't replace it? Well, she ended up in the Juvenile Detention Center (JDC) because she put Mary in the hospital for a long time during that raid. We all hated that the girl had to leave because she was nice and didn't keep up mess like some of these other girls, plus she ended up being my roommate because both of our roommates had left so we asked if she could move into my room. The supervisor okayed it.

Anyways, she had left and a new girl was moving in. Her name was Blanche Blaque Blaze. The girls called her BB. She was 16 years old and was originally from Jamaica but moved here when she turned 1 years old. She had a nice accent and her skin would turn this gorgeous reddish color in the summertime. She seemed like a cool teen at first, but like Ms. Lishay told you we all go through a honeymoon phase (even though I didn't, lol. Just kidding!) When BB moved into my room she showed me all of this cool stuff that she had. She had a lot of gold and silver bracelets, necklaces, rings and watches. She had all kinds of little knick knacks and trinkets. She told me all these stories about how she traveled to different places and got these souvenirs from each place she had traveled to.

One Friday night, one of the staff left her purse open on the office table. BB asked the staff if she could use the phone to talk to her caseworker and the staff said yes. If we are calling our attorney, CASA worker, or caseworker we can use the office phone for privacy but if we are calling anyone else we have to use the phone in the hallway. BB called her caseworker and talked to her for about 30 minutes and then came back into the room very excited about something. I asked her what she was so excited about and she said, "My caseworker is coming by to drop off my clothing money." We all had different caseworkers and some of us received clothing vouchers while others received cash money.

An hour later BB's caseworker came by and handed her an envelope. BB hugged her caseworker and told her thanks. Her caseworker told her to let her know how it goes. I didn't want to seem like I was nosy so I didn't ask her why her caseworker had said that. Two hours went by and we heard one of the staff scream. We all rushed to the staff office to see what was going on and the staff was in the office crying.

Tasha went into the office and asked the staff what happened and she said, "It's gone. It's gone. Someone stole it from me."

Tasha asked her, "Stole what?"

The staff replied, "Someone stole my check money. I just cashed my check and the money is gone."

Tasha told us, "Ok, everyone go back to what you were doing."

So I sat at the dining room table because the staff office was right behind it and read a book (while I was trying to hear what staff was saying.) The staff kept saying it was in my purse when I walked in here. Tasha asked the staff where did she have her purse and if she had left it open. The staff told her it has been sitting in the same spot since I came in and that it was open. The staff had left her purse by the phone. Tasha told the staff that she could never leave her purse out and that we have lockers for a reason. Tasha told her that they were going to have to conduct a room search but that she should not get her hopes up because they might not find it.

Tasha asked the staff if any youths had been in the office. One of the staff informed Tasha that BB had asked to use the phone and that she allowed her to call her caseworker. Tasha came out of the office and said that they were doing a random room search. Don't get me wrong they did room searches all of the time but we were hoping and praying that BB didn't take her money because that meant that we had another thief in the house and she was my roommate.

Tasha and that staff searched my

room while other staff searched the other girls' rooms. Tasha lifted up BB's bed and saw a lot of twenty dollar bills under it. Tasha asked the staff how much was it and the staff told her. It was the exact amount under BB's bed. Everyone was in shock. Tasha asked BB why she stole the staff money and BB told her that she didn't steal anything and that her caseworker had given her that money.

Tasha was smart and hip to the games that some of the girls played. Tasha called BB's caseworker and asked her if she gave her any money and if so how much. BB's caseworker told Tasha that she had dropped off a permission form for a job and that she didn't give her any money. Now it made sense. Because when BB's caseworker left, she said, "Let me know how it goes." Tasha got upset and asked BB again why did she take the staff's money out of her purse. BB told her, "The bitch left her purse open so that meant that she didn't want it. If you leave something out that means you don't want it and you don't care about it." Tasha had to hold the staff back because she looked like she was going to choke BB to death.

If there was one thing that the staff and we girls agreed on it was that we didn't like the fact that there was a thief in the house because that meant we had to constantly watch our stuff. After that, a month had gone by and it seemed like that stealing thing was a one-time thing. Boy was I wrong. One morning I was getting ready to go to school and I couldn't find my locket that my mother had given me a very long time ago. I didn't think anything about it and I just had thought I misplaced it in my room somewhere. I rushed to get in the line and told myself that I would find it when I got back home. So when I got back home and I still couldn't find it I got upset. It was BB and my laundry day so I waited until BB went to the laundry mat to check her stuff. Do you know the girl had my locket in her jewelry box? I was so mad and I told Ms. Lishay and Tasha.

Tasha asked me why I went through BB's stuff instead of telling her.

I said, "Because I didn't want to accuse her of taking it if she didn't."

Tasha stated that she understood, but that I still should have come to her first.

Tasha had asked all of the other girls to look through their stuff and make sure nothing was missing. Every girl in the house had something missing. Tasha went into the girl's room and laid everything she had out on the bed, the floor, and the table and one by one had the girls look through the stuff and get their belongings; we had to do this every month because BB kept stealing stuff.

During lunch, we all talked about what we should do the next time it happened because BB had began stealing our stuff and putting it with another girl's belongings in the house. She had us all losing our minds and turning on each other. But we knew it had to be something because before she came everything was nice and peaceful. We were determined to get the peace back. Long story short, we ended up jumping BB because we had had enough. She finally messed with the wrong girl in the house and took something that was extremely sentimental to her and messed it up. The girl lost it. We all jumped in and whooped her ass, too. It was so funny because Lyla took off her shoe and was beating BB with it. At times Lyla acted like our mom and would talk and act like a mother would.

Needless to say, after that, BB never stole anything from us again. A few months after that, BB ended up getting hospitalized because she tried to steal something from a different staff and the staff went into BB's room and took her jewelry box and told BB, "You left it out so it must mean you didn't want it." BB chased that staff around the house with a pair of scissors and told her that she was going to stab her to death if she didn't give it back to her. Sometimes it can be like comedy central over here. I swear, lol.

Chapter 10
The fight within...

At the age of 14 years old I decided that I didn't want to have anything else to do with men. Yes, I am gay, and I don't give a fuck what anybody has to say. Men are ugly, dirty, and nasty and all they want to do is fuck you and use you. If I could kill them all I would. One of the staff members said I should not say that, but they don't get it. Everything that has happened to me has been because of a fucked up, nasty, smelly man. I can never have kids because of a stupid, nasty man. So anyone who tells me I'm wrong is a stupid ass person.

I'm just a teenager and I feel like my life is over. When we go to the mall (staff has to take us once a month so that we can buy clothes, hygiene products, etc.) and I see other teenagers laughing with their friends, buying expensive stuff, driving their nice cars, and telling their parents how much they love them or thanking them for buying them something, I get pissed. I don't understand what in the hell makes them so much better than me. What makes them more suitable and worthy for that lifestyle than me. Is what my mother said true? Did my maker look at me and say, "This is one ugly kid. Put her over there with the fucked up people."

    I didn't ask to be here. I didn't ask to be used as a sex slave. I didn't ask to be fucked up like this. As a child, you hear people say all the time you can be anything when you grow up. My question to them is how can you be anything when you grew up in hell and have to take six different psychotropic meds just to feel and act somewhat normal and eight different meds to treat STDs? I don't have no "connections" because I am rich and beautiful. Why do I even want to be alive? When I read statistics about individuals like myself, there is nothing positive and uplifting. When have you ever turned on your television and saw a black woman with a horrible background say, "I made it!" Look at me and what I had to go through. Now, I am a doctor who has a wonderful spouse with two adopted kids." When have you seen a commercial like that or a show like that, or anything like that? Never and you never will. The only time the spotlight is ever on us is when rich people want regular people to think they are good because they gave thousands to a shelter or some overseas orphanage who show the African kids with the big stomachs suffering.

That's the only time you hear something about kids like me. Other than that, people want to block us out or act like we don't exist because they don't want to feel bad. Wow, I will never understand. Maybe if I make it to heaven God will be able to tell me why I had to go through all of this. Or, what I did that was so bad that a guy was allowed to ruin my cervix to the point that I will never be able to have kids. All I want is to understand. That's it. I just want to understand. (Raven was in tears as she cried herself to sleep after writing this.)

Chapter 11

Safe...

The only good thing that I can say about Safe Haven is that I have met a few people who have gone out of their way trying to help me. One of those persons is my therapist. I know as a black person I was taught that the only people who went to a therapist were crazy people and white rich people who have money to throw away. But my therapist has helped me to open up and realize that no matter how bad my life appears to be someone else has it 10 times harder than me. She also has helped me to realize that there are people who actually care about me and that there are people who will accept me for who I am.

During my time at Safe Haven, a lot of stuff has happened from us having wild parties on top of the gym that we got in trouble for. Then there were the raids we had in which the staff that we didn't like got beat down for treating us like shit or made us lie on our peers so that they would not get into trouble. Staff members around here do all types of things that they know they should not be doing, from having sex with some of the kids to buying and selling drugs to the kids. Yes, you heard me right. But when some of the girls try to tell management what happened nothing happens. We could have proof that a particular staff sexually abused us and the evidence would disappear.

The saddest thing that ever happened here is one of the girls being sexually abused by a staff member. She thought he really cared about her and was going to be there for her. Once she got out, she found out that that staff member already had a girlfriend that he was engaged to. When she found out that this staff member just wanted to have sex with her, she lost it and went into her bedroom, put on her graduation dress, and hung herself in her closet. She was such a beautiful girl who had a beautiful personality. But she had been hurt a lot throughout her life and this was the last straw. Everyone loved her around here because she was the one who always told you not to worry and that everything would work itself out. She kept us encouraged when we wanted to give up.

It's so crazy how quickly your world can change and leave you questioning everything. If it wasn't for my therapist I don't think I would have made it through her death because everything became gray. But my therapist, as she likes to say, "Pulled me through it." My therapist was there when I picked out my Independent Living Options (ILO) placement. She was there when I had doubts about my relationship with my girlfriend. She was there for me when I found out that I got accepted to Columbia College.

I ran into my therapist on Facebook like three years later and she asked me what has been going on. I was so excited to tell her. I told her that my girlfriend and I moved in together and adopted a puppy. I told her that because of my past I work with troubled inner-city teens who have given up on life. She informed me that if I needed help with anything to let her know. Yep, that was my therapist always there when you needed her. She was always there to let you know that someone on this planet really loves you and cares about you.

Well, my name is Raven and I am happy to be a part of the *Group Home Drama* book series. I can't wait until you meet the other incredible girls who overcame their struggles just like I did due to certain individuals like our therapist who refused to give up on us. Some of our stories will make you cry, while others will make you laugh. But in the end, our goal is to help other young girls out there who are going through hard times realize that there is a purpose for your life even though you might not be able to see it at this time.

Chapter 12

The Here and Now...

The present me …. At the time, I thought that I was going to die if anything else happened. But I can honestly say that my girlfriend and I are happy. We absolutely adore our dog Andy and are getting ready to plan a trip. We want to go to Hawaii because neither one of us has really been out of the state of Illinois. Once we get back from our trip we are going to be traveling to different states to see what it would be like to live there. My girlfriend and I have both agreed that if we find a place that we fall in love with that we are going to move. I think that is going to be great.

A couple of years after I moved into the ILO program I contacted that worker. Can you believe she stills works there?

Well, I couldn't. I just knew I was going to call her and get that message. "Ding, Ding, Ding, the number you have dialed is either out of service ... please try your call again later." But no, she answered and on top of all of that remembered who I was. She gave me the names of some of the relatives on my father's side as well as their addresses and phone numbers. Even though I had second thoughts about calling them after all of these years my girlfriend convinced me to call them.

So I spoke with one of my aunts who invited me to their family reunion where I met my father's entire family. They were so nice to me and my girlfriend. We laughed and cried and laughed and cried some more. My father's aunt told me a lot of stuff about my father and how I reminded her of him. She asked me why I never reached out to her while I was at Safe Haven and I told her that, for the most part, I was scared of being rejected by my father's family. I told her that at that time I was not strong enough to deal with another negative blow.

My father's aunt Anna May stated that she understood and that she had been telling the rest of the family that I would come around when I was good and ready to. Anna May was right because I did. My girlfriend and I now attend the family reunion every year and Anna May has put us on the Reunion Committee so now we get to plan where the reunion will be, what we will eat, and what the theme will be. We really love being a part of that. After everything that I went through I honestly thought that I was going to be dead by now. If you would have told me then that one day I was going to be planning a trip to Hawaii, having a wonderful relationship with my father's family, and having a wonderful girlfriend who has been by my side since we met, I probably would have kicked your fucking ass and yelled at you to get the fuck out of my face with that bull shit.

What else can I tell you? Well, I still journal every night. Why? Because, if and when the critical tape starts playing in my head, it's one of the tools that I use to pause the critical tape. I let my hair grow back. It's shoulder length now, but I keep it braided. I have lost weight. I am now around 100 pounds. Remember, I am 5'1" so if I am any size bigger, I will look fat. Because of my job, I don't dress so tomboyish anymore. Don't get me wrong I won't be caught dead in a dress or skirt, but I think my current style is more age appropriate and professional.

I was diagnosed with depression and bi-polar disorders while at Safe Haven, and Ms. Lishay got me on the right prescription regimen. As Ms. Lishay loves to say, "I am able to pause the critical tape now." Remember the self-harming behavior that I had back then? Relax, I didn't relapse or anything. I have never gone back to the drugs or the inserting.

After my girlfriend and I finished traveling, we are going to take classes to become foster parents so that we can help other girls like us see that there is a way out of the darkness. I told my girlfriend that she can get pregnant if she wants to but she said that if we couldn't do it together that she didn't want to do it. She also said that there are too many kids out here that have been abused, traumatized, and ready to give up on life that need someone to help them.

Remember the photo album that the worker dropped off after my mother died? Well, my girlfriend and I finally looked at everything that was in the photo album. My girlfriend and I cried a lot because there were a lot of pictures of my parents and me before my dad passed away. At times, I still wonder why my parents had to die the way that they did. I also wonder how close my sibling and I would have been. Would we have loved the same things? Would my sibling even like me? Would my sibling have turned out like me? Who would my sibling favor - my mother or my father? Sometimes I also wonder if my father was still living how close we would be. Would I have been a daddy's little girl? But when my mind goes to this place of wonder and questions, my girlfriend is always there to help me through. She also makes sure that I journal all of the stuff that I am thinking about.

I am in agreement with her. Ms. Lishay always said that if we are able to help someone else to do it because helping someone in need is a blessing in itself. I know one thing though - if we have any issues with these foster kids that we don't know how to handle we will be contacting Ms. Lishay and she is already aware of this, lol. If you're wondering why we are okay with Ms. Lishay writing these books it's because I wish there was a book series like this when I was lying on those tracks. If there was I never would have been on those tracks. I know there are other youth (like Ms. Lishay likes to call us) out there who have been through the same thing I have or worst things than I have and will need these books just to get through each day.

I asked Ms. Lishay if she could at least tell me or give me a hint as to what her next book is going to be about and she told me that the next book is going to be a girl who everyone in the home really cared about. She was really nice and had been through a hell of a lot of shit. Ms. Lishay said that she was calling the girl Alyssa.

(Ms. Lishay: The one thing that I will tell you about Alyssa is that the beginning of her story is going to make you cry but if you could see her now, Superstar...)

For further information,

contact the author at:

Elite Life Skills

E-mail address: mclishay@elitelifeskills.com

Web site address:
www.elitelifeskills.com/gdhs/raven.html

If you would like to obtain an autographed

picture from the author, please send an email to:

autograph@elitelifeskills.com.

For release dates on the

Group Home Drama Series,

please go to:

www.elitelifeskills.com/ghds/releasedates.html

Check out upcoming book contests on our web site,
www.elitelifeskills.com/ghds/contests.html.

Also, become an Elite Warrior at
www.elitelifeskills.com/ghds/elitewarrior.html and

start making a difference with our youth!